Praise for …

Erasing Hell

"*Erasing Hell* is an extraordinarily important book. Francis Chan speaks with trembling and compassion. He recognizes this debate is about God, His nature, and His authority. At stake is whether or not we will trust Him. Francis lays his heart on the table; I was not only informed, but moved. It's rare that a book mixes straight-from-the-heart talk with diligent citation of Scripture. *Erasing Hell* is highly readable yet goes deep and into detail exactly when it needs to. Preston Sprinkle's research and Francis Chan's presentation are a dynamic combination. This remarkable book embraces not what, in pride, we want to believe, but what, in humility, we must believe. My heartfelt thanks to Francis Chan for taking us to God's Word in a Christlike spirit of grace and truth. And for calling on us not to apologize for God, but to apologize *to* God for presuming to be wiser and more loving than our Savior."

Randy Alcorn, author of *Heaven* and *If God Is Good*

"It's time for the H word. A lot of people go through hell on earth, but what if there is also a hell *after* earth? Hell's stock has fallen off lately from lack of public confidence, but how can thousands, perhaps millions, reject hell as a myth and yet still believe in heaven and cherish fond hopes of going there? Surely if we hate suffering, God must hate it worse and could never have founded an institution as horrible as described in Dante's *Inferno*. But the same Jesus who gave heaven a five-star rating also described an otherworldly chamber of horrors. Who goes there and why? And for how long? In *Erasing Hell*, my good friend Francis Chan takes a close look at some tough, frightening questions … and his answers may honestly surprise you!"

Joni Eareckson Tada, Joni and Friends International Disability Center

"Everyone needs to read *Erasing Hell* by Francis Chan and Preston Sprinkle. Chan and Sprinkle accurately and clearly reflect the biblical teaching on heaven, hell, and eternal destiny. They provide a timely reminder that we don't define God, but He reveals Himself to us in the pages of Scripture."

Tremper Longman, Robert H. Gundry Professor of Biblical Studies at
Westmont College and author of *Reading the Bible with Heart and Mind*

"Francis Chan and Preston Sprinkle raise the questions we all have about this very critical topic and respond with biblical integrity and a commitment to truth, as well as incredible compassion for people. *Erasing Hell* is an extremely important and much-needed book."

Dan Kimball, pastor and author of *They Like Jesus but Not the Church*

"Francis holds the fine line between committed biblical faithfulness and a deep compassion for people and refuses to create a false dichotomy between the two. He feels the weight and horror of the reality of hell and yet avoids the error of lapsing into mere humanism, all the while providing a well-reasoned defense for the view of Scripture on the subject. I am so thankful for this book, as will you be."

Britt Merrick, pastor of Reality Santa Barbara

"Recent works by evangelicals on the postmortem future(s) of humanity have raised important questions and brought some sobering and uncomfortable issues to the fore. Chan and Sprinkle provide a remarkable service to the church by engaging these issues with courage, clarity, and grace. This book is a model of careful biblical scholarship, providing fresh light from the Jewish context of the New Testament. They also write as pastors seeking to provide wisdom for ministry, enabling the people of God to embody the love of God for the world."

Timothy Gombis, associate professor of New Testament
at Grand Rapids Theological Seminary

stoperasinghell

preston sprinkle
with francis chan

stoperasinghell

an interactive workbook
for individual or
small-group study

David C Cook®
transforming lives together

STOP ERASING HELL
Published by David C Cook
4050 Lee Vance View
Colorado Springs, CO 80918 U.S.A.

David C Cook Distribution Canada
55 Woodslee Avenue, Paris, Ontario, Canada N3L 3E5

David C Cook U.K., Kingsway Communications
Eastbourne, East Sussex BN23 6NT, England

The graphic circle C logo is a registered trademark of David C Cook.

LCCN 2011944721
ISBN 978-0-7814-0815-8
eISBN 978-0-7814-0829-5

The Team: Don Pape, Alex Field, Amy Konyndyk, Nick Lee, Caitlyn York, Karen Athen
Cover Design: Jim Elliston

Printed in the United States of America
First Edition 2012

1 2 3 4 5 6 7 8 9 10

122011

Contents

Getting Started

Most Christians believe in hell. They believe that hell is a place of never-ending punishment for those who don't love Christ. They believe that it's real, that it's not a myth, and that many people will go there—even some of their loved ones.

But few of these same Christians live in light of this belief. In all honesty, much of my own daily routine shows little evidence that I believe in a place of torment called hell. I come into contact with many people throughout my day. Sometimes I speak to thousands of people at a time. But rarely does the reality of hell shape the way I live and speak in any significant way.

I pray that this workbook will help change this—both in you and in me. So this workbook is intended to do two things:

One: to help you understand what the Bible actually says about hell. Many people have presuppositions about hell, so it'll be important to dig into the Bible to see what *it* actually says. At times this will take hard work, since some passages aren't as clear as many people think. To get the most out of this study, you will need to approach each session with a desire to think long and hard through some of these passages. Paul told Timothy to be "a worker who has no need to be ashamed, rightly handling the word of truth" (2 Tim. 2:15). Ezra "set his heart to study the Law of the LORD" (Ezra 7:10). The same zeal to understand what the Bible says is necessary for studying the doctrine of hell.

Two: to help you live differently in light of what the Bible teaches. Ezra didn't just "set his heart to study the Law of the LORD"—according to the rest of the verse, he studied it in order "to do it" (Ezra 7:10). Obedience must flow from studying the Bible. This may seem kind of weird in a study of *hell*. How do we obey this doctrine? But as you will quickly see, the reality of hell has many implications for how we as Christians are to live. Like all doctrines, the biblical teaching on hell is designed to affect not just our minds but—most of all—our hearts and lives. After Paul gave his most intense description of hell (2 Thess. 1:5–10), he turned right around and prayed that "our God may make you worthy of his calling and may fulfill every resolve for good and every work of faith by his power" (2 Thess. 1:11). Obedience should flow from doctrine.

Paul's prayer for the Thessalonian believers is my prayer for you. I pray that God would use this study to transform both your mind and your life, and that He would "make you worthy of his calling" as a result of this study.

How to Get the Most Out of This Workbook

There are a few different ways to use this workbook. You can work through the study as an individual, as a part of a small group, or even during a weekend retreat. I've made some suggestions for using the workbook in each of these settings below.

This workbook is designed to work hand in hand with the *Erasing Hell* book. Ideally, you will read the relevant chapter from *Erasing Hell*, then go through the corresponding session in the workbook. But while that is the most thorough way of studying the material, the workbook also stands on its own. You'll notice that each session refers to the book, and some questions ask you to interact with paragraphs from the book, but you can get a lot out of this workbook even if you haven't read *Erasing Hell*.

Using the Workbook on Your Own

The most effective way to use this workbook is to go through it on your own, even if you're also going to discuss it as a group or on a retreat. Many of the questions are personal, and taking the time to read through the sessions and think through how each question should affect your life will give the study depth and immediate personal application. Again, it would be best if you read the relevant chapter in *Erasing Hell* before you worked through the corresponding session in the workbook.

Using the Workbook in a Small Group

If you're working through the material as a part of a small group, the best way to begin is by working through each chapter on your own before the group discussion (see the section for individuals above). Reading and thinking through each session on your own before your group meets will better prepare you for the discussion. I recommend writing in your answers and any notes or questions you may have before you meet with your group, and then adding to your notes based on the discussion.

When you meet with your group, I recommend establishing a discussion leader. (If you've been chosen for this task, see the "Notes for Discussion Leaders" at the end of this workbook.) This person doesn't need to have all the answers. The discussion leader will simply guide the conversation and decide when to move on to the next question.

For each session, discuss the numbered questions as a group. Some of the questions can be answered quickly, but I encourage you to take your time, giving multiple group members a chance to share. This will enrich the discussion, and different perspectives will often give you more ideas for practical application.

Most importantly, I encourage you to be honest with the members of your group. Hell is a difficult doctrine to study, and it should be expected that some—if not most—in the group may have difficultly believing that God will send people to hell. You will get the most out of this study if people feel the freedom to be honest with how they respond to the doctrine. At the end of the day, we all must align our beliefs with what God says in the Bible, but sometimes this takes time. And there's no virtue in rattling off the "right" answer out of fear that others in the group will judge you. If your desire is to grow and change, you will need to create an arena where people feel the freedom to be honest, so that the group members can speak into one another's lives. By opening up to one another, your whole group will become more open to the Spirit's leading.

Using the Workbook for a Weekend Retreat

Some churches will want to use this workbook as a part of a weekend retreat. If that's the case, I recommend dividing the large group into smaller groups and setting aside seven different small-group meeting times. Small groups of four to six people give everyone a chance to talk. People who are shy about talking in large groups are often more comfortable talking in small ones. And people who tend to dominate discussions in large groups are more easily balanced out by others in small circles.

You'll probably want to address the entire group at least a few times during the weekend to give them some thoughts, but giving them time to meet in smaller groups will be important. Group members will want to read the section for small groups above, and discussion leaders will want to read the "Notes for Discussion Leaders" section at the end of this workbook.

Discussion leaders don't need to be experts, either in the content or in leading groups, because they will fairly quickly learn how to guide a conversation with only four to six other people. Ideally, you will choose discussion leaders ahead of time, but if you can't, it's surprising how often these groups can choose the most natural leader among them after getting to know one another for only a brief time. You can read aloud the job description of a discussion leader (see the end of this workbook) and pray for the Holy Spirit to guide the groups in choosing discussion leaders. Groups will often unanimously choose someone among them to do the job once they know what it involves. As for the members of the group, it's better for them to stick with the same group for the whole series, so that they get to know each other.

SESSION 1

Does Everyone Go to Heaven?

For more information on the material in this session, read the preface and chapter 1 of the book Erasing Hell: What God Said about Eternity, and the Things We Made Up.

Heaven and *hell* are familiar terms for Christians and non-Christians alike, especially if you live in an English-speaking country. The words appear in movies, in television shows, on the radio. Sometimes they are used as swear words (especially *hell*), spouted off flippantly upon hearing a piece of bad news. We use them as empty modifiers in everyday speech. Instead of saying "no," we say "*heavens* no" just to get our point across. Needless to say, the words *heaven* and *hell* have lost their biblical richness through overuse. All the more need to understand precisely what we mean when we talk about heaven—and hell.

This workbook is a study of hell. And before we get started, it's important to realize the seriousness of the subject. We are not studying a natural catastrophe, a violent war, a fatal disease, or any other so-called "hells on earth." This life brings much tragedy and suffering—but nothing we experience in this life compares to the heart-wrenching misery that will accompany the place we are studying in this book. This study is a sober one. You will find no jokes or cute stories to make the doctrine of hell more palatable. But this is a study that will change your life forever. You don't have to meditate on the reality of hell for very long before you begin to live differently in light of it.

Before we go deeper, I want to ask three questions up front. And I really want you to be honest with your answers.

1. Without looking at the Bible, list all the characteristics about hell that you can. For example, you can describe what it is like, or who will go there, or where it is located. If you don't know much of what the Bible says about hell, just describe what you have heard about it.

2. Now, in light of your previous answer, describe what this view says about God. If hell is the way you've portrayed it, then what does your perspective teach us about God?

3. Lastly—and be honest here—what are the hardest things for you to believe about hell? These may include logical problems or emotional difficulties that you have when you think about hell. What makes it difficult for you to believe that God would send people to hell?

Hell is not an easy doctrine to swallow. If you listed quite a few things in question 3, that's okay. I have a long list myself! This is why I begin *Erasing Hell* with the line: "If you are excited to read this book, you have issues." It's true. Hell is not something we must delight in and love to talk about. After all, even God said that He does not delight in the death of the wicked (Ezek. 33:11).

But if hell is real—*if* the Bible says that there is a real place of punishment for those who don't love Jesus—then we must take God at His word. We must embrace what God has said about Himself and His plan of justice, even when it is difficult to believe. This is what our study here is all about. Yes, it's a book about hell. But even more, it's a book about God. So before going any further, take a brief moment and ask God to answer the following prayers:

Heavenly Father …

- Help me to embrace You more firmly and cherish You more fervently by understanding Your Word more.
- Prevent my emotions or mere human logic from clouding my view of hell.
- Open up my heart to Your ways and Your character. Give me eyes to see and ears to hear, so that Your ways become my own.
- Kindle afresh in my heart and mind a higher view of who You are. And may my life be radically transformed by a fresh encounter with You through this study.

Next, we need to talk about the possibility of an after-death conversion. I suspect that you may have wondered about this. Every Christian believes that God accepts sinners who repent and turn to Christ *in this life*. This is a cardinal truth. But does this invitation extend beyond death? Will unbelievers have a chance to "get saved" after they die? This question is an important one, because if there are second chances after death, then the reality of hell is not nearly as important. Plus, there are a growing number of Christians who believe that God's invitation to follow Jesus extends beyond the grave.

But what does the Bible say? This will be a question that permeates this workbook. Regardless of what we think or what we've always been taught, *what does the Bible actually say* about the matter? Does the Bible hold out hope that God will give unbelievers a second chance to believe in Jesus after death?

Chapter 1 of *Erasing Hell* discusses a few passages that *seem to say* God will save everyone in the end. One of the difficulties in interpreting these passages is the meaning of the word *all.* For instance, 1 Corinthians 15:22 says, "In Christ shall *all* be made alive." By itself, this verse could mean that everyone will end up being saved, but the context doesn't support this interpretation. Paul was clearly thinking about the resurrection of *believers* ("those who belong to Christ" in 15:23). Basically, 15:22–23 says that all who belong to Christ will be made alive at His coming.

4. Do you find it persuasive that "all" in this case doesn't mean "every single person who ever lived"? Explain. (You may want to have a look at pages 26–33 of *Erasing Hell*, along with 1 Cor. 15:20–26; Phil. 2:9–11; Rev. 21:24–25.)

Another difficult passage is 1 Timothy 2:4, which says that God "wants all people to be saved" (ISV). If God "wants" all people to be saved, then this raises the question: *Does God get what He wants?* But Scripture talks about two different kinds "wills" of God, His "wanting" something to happen: the *moral* will of God and the *decreed* will of God.

5. Explain the difference between God's moral will and His decreed will. It may help to go back and read how these are distinguished in the life of Samson (page 32 of *Erasing Hell*).

Studying the Bible can be hard work! Some passages are easy to understand, while others demand much more time and reflection, or even some time in Greek dictionaries. But when we're studying, we need to make sure that our goal is not to win an argument or just to have good doctrine. Our end goal of all Bible study is to love God and love people more—even when we are sorting out difficult doctrines, like the *moral* and *decreed* will of God!

With that in mind, let's bring this back to the practical level. In *Erasing Hell*, I argue that the word *all* often means "all *types*" of people. So in 1 Timothy 2, Paul reminds Timothy that God even wants pedophile maniacs like Caesar Nero ("kings and all who are in high positions"—1 Tim. 2:2) to repent and come to Jesus. God is in the business of loving and saving sinners—especially the really bad ones!

6. Is there anyone in your life who you feel is beyond the reaches of God's grace? You may not verbally admit this, but deep down you feel that there is no chance this person will come to Jesus. Write down the name of this person (or people) below, and pray for him or her.

7. What are some things you could do to show this person (or these people) that God loves him or her?

The church is a multiethnic, multiage, multiclass body of redeemed sinners. God loves this diversity because God loves *all types of people*. This seems to be the main point of passages like 1 Timothy 2:4 and 2 Peter 3:9.

8. Is there anyone in your life (Christian or not) whom you have not loved the way God loves? This may be a person of a different ethnicity, language, social class, or age.

God extends the offer of salvation to all types of people—but the offer is only available in this life. There is nothing in the Bible that suggests that unbelievers will have a chance to accept Jesus after they die. In fact, Luke 13:22–30 says clearly that a time will come when the door of salvation will be closed and people will have no more opportunities to turn to Jesus.

Go back and read through this passage. Read it *slowly*. Meditate on it. Jesus doesn't tell this parable to prove that people will go to hell, but to challenge His followers to live different lives. Rather than arguing that the door will be closed, we need to live differently while that door is open!

9. Even though Luke 13:22–30 never mentions the word *hell*, Jesus uses a phrase in this passage that He uses elsewhere when describing hell. This phrase is *weeping and gnashing of teeth*. What do you think it means?

10. What do you think Jesus means when He says, "I do not know where you come from" (Luke 13:25)?

11. Jesus told His parables not only to challenge our intellects but to grip our emotions. As you read through Luke 13:22–30, what emotions does this story raise in you? Does it make you fearful? Sad? Scared?

Luke 13:22–30 is a tough parable to meditate on. I often picture friends and family who don't know Christ, on the outside knocking, begging for Jesus to let them in. Again, God gave us this parable to change the way we think, feel, and act throughout our daily routine. So pray that God would use the reality of hell to transform the way you live—that He would use this study to help shape your life and thinking so that it looks more like Christ.

Reflections on ...
Does Everyone Go to Heaven?

SESSION 2

Has Hell Changed? Or Have We?

For more information on the material in this session, read chapter 2 of the book **Erasing Hell: What God Said about Eternity, and the Things We Made Up.**

We live in an image-saturated culture. Pictures are everywhere. They're on billboards, on magazines; they fill our TV screens and cover our walls. Most societies (especially America) are inundated with images. And images often reflect what we want to see. They reflect who we are. So when we create images of Jesus—in paintings, in children's books, or in movies—we often portray Him in our own image. In America, Jesus is often portrayed as good looking, fit, and white. He has long flowing hair, an impeccable complexion, and a thin bone structure. His appearance is based on what we want Him to look like and not the way He actually would have appeared.

We do the same with Jesus' words. We often interpret Jesus' words in light of what we want Him to say, not in light of what He actually said. It's so easy for us to read Jesus' words in light of our own culture rather than His. This is especially true with what He says about hell. In chapter 2 of *Erasing Hell*, I examine the first-century world of Jesus. This is a very important discussion because it helps us understand Jesus in light of His own culture and context. Jesus used words, imagery, and parables that were familiar to the first-century Jews, the people He was addressing. So to understand what He said about hell, it's important to put ourselves in the sandals of the first-century Jews. We want to understand Jesus the way His original audience would have understood Him, and not how *we want* to understand Him. We must read Jesus in His own context.

1. Does it matter to you that Jesus was a first-century Jew and probably wasn't a light-skinned guy with long flowing hair? Explain.

2. Jesus didn't necessarily agree with His contemporaries about hell, but let's start there. How would you describe the view of hell depicted in this well-known writing from Jesus' day?

> [T]he chambers shall give up the souls which have been committed to them. And the Most High shall be revealed upon the seat of judgment ... recompense shall follow ... unrighteous deeds shall not sleep. Then the pit of torment shall appear ... and the furnace of Gehenna shall be disclosed. (first century AD)[1]

---

1. 4 Ezra 7:32–36.

3. If most of Jesus' audience believed hell was a place of punishment for the wicked, and Jesus thought they were wrong, how would you expect Him to address that? Why?

4. When Jesus' contemporaries talked about hell, they mainly used imagery of fire, darkness, and lamenting. What do you think these images are meant to convey about hell?

5. From what you know of Jesus, how would you expect Him to respond when Jewish teachers used such imagery?

6. Jews in Jesus' day thought hell would involve either annihilation or never-ending punishment. What is annihilation? How is it different from never-ending torment of conscious people?

7. Does it matter to you how long the suffering in hell lasts—whether it's a quick destruction or a never-ending torment? Explain.

We've looked at three main things first-century Jews believed about hell:

- Hell is a place of punishment after judgment.
- Hell is described in imagery of fire and darkness, where people lament.
- Hell is a place of annihilation or never-ending punishment.

Now, you may have heard the theory that hell (Greek: *gehenna*) originally referred to a garbage dump outside Jerusalem. I personally grew up thinking this, and I still hear it in sermons and read about it in books. But after studying the meaning of the Greek word *gehenna*, I was surprised to find out that it was not a garbage dump. In fact, as I explain in chapter 2 of *Erasing Hell*, this theory arose in the Middle Ages (around AD 1200) and probably was not what Jesus had in mind when He spoke of hell.

8. If you have a copy of the book handy, explain why it is unlikely that "hell" (*gehenna*) referred to a garbage dump.

9. On page 61 in the book, I explain how the Hinnon Valley (from which we get the word *gehenna*) became associated with hell. How did this valley become known as a place of punishment?

10. How would thinking of hell as just a garbage dump be different from thinking of it as a place of punishment, fire, darkness, and lament?

11. What questions has this discussion raised in your mind?

The church today doesn't often talk about God's wrath and judgment. These concepts are not very attractive, and yet first-century Jews didn't shrink back from preaching about God's judgment of people in hell. And, as we will see, Jesus was a first-century Jew, and He also wasn't reluctant to talk about hell and judgment.

12. Are you comfortable talking about hell with an unbeliever? Why, or why not?

13. What are some ways in which hell can be talked about *wrongly*?

14. What are some ways to talk about hell to an unbeliever that still manifest Christian love?

Understanding the historical background of the New Testament is important for correct interpretation. But it's easy to get caught up in the facts of history and miss the point of the text: to transform us into Christ-likeness. As we move into the New Testament for the next three sessions, I want to emphasize again that hell is not just a doctrine to be discussed and debated. The very reality of hell is designed to shape us into Christ-likeness. Before you begin the next session, pray that God would help you understand and embrace what the Bible says about hell. And also, pray that God would form you into the image of Christ as a result of learning what Jesus and the apostles said about hell.

Reflections on ...
Has Hell Changed? Or Have We?

SESSION 3

What Jesus Actually Said about Hell

For more information on the material in this session, read chapter 3 of the book **Erasing Hell: What God Said about Eternity, and the Things We Made Up.**

Studying the Bible can be hard work. But we need to make sure that it doesn't become a mere academic exercise. God gave us the Bible—and all the truths in it, including hell—in order to shape us into Christ-likeness. In session 1, I encouraged you to acquire a more passionate heart for the lost through this study. You probably know several people, some of whom are very close to you, who are on their way to hell. And this should stir up more zeal in you to reach out to them, to love and serve them more, and to continue to pray for them and tell them about Jesus.

I hope fervent evangelism will be an outcome of this study. I also pray that God would instill in you a healthy sense of fear. Not that we should be scared of God. After all, we are covered by the blood of Christ! But the Bible still demands that we have a deep-seated reverential awe of our King. Isaiah put it like this: "But this is the one to whom I will look: he who is humble and contrite in spirit and trembles at my word" (Isa. 66:2). As you continue to study the doctrine of hell, pray that God would humble you in the process. Understand that the only reason why you are not headed there—if you are a genuine believer—is God's grace. Therefore, tremble as you read the words of Jesus that we will discuss in this session. He is the all-sovereign King of Creation. And He has *spoken* so that we might *tremble*.

Chapters 2 and 3 of *Erasing Hell* are closely related. I tried to situate Jesus in His own historical and cultural context. After surveying the Jewish view of hell, I said at the beginning of chapter 3, "If Jesus rejected the widespread Jewish belief in hell—then He would certainly need to be clear about this" (page 73). This is an important point to understand.

1. How do you respond to this statement: "If Jesus rejected the widespread Jewish belief in hell—then He would certainly need to be clear about this." Do you agree? Disagree? Why?

In the chapter, I argue that, far from challenging what His fellow Jews believed about hell, Jesus talked about hell in the very same ways:

- Hell is a place of punishment after judgment.
- Hell is described in imagery of fire and darkness, where people lament.
- Hell is a place of annihilation or never-ending punishment.

2. *(Optional)* If you want to examine for yourself what Jesus said about hell, here is a list of all of the passages where He used the word *gehenna* (hell) as well as some others where He alluded to hell. You can look them up on your own, or if you're meeting with a group, you can divide into two or three teams and assign some passages to each team. Ask the teams to answer this question and then report back to the group:

How closely do these passages match up with the three statements about hell that are listed above? Highlight the ways each passage does or doesn't fit that picture.

Passages that name hell:

Matthew 5:21–22

Matthew 5:29–30

Matthew 10:28

Matthew 18:7–9

Matthew 23:15, 33

Mark 9:42–48

Luke 12:4–10

Passages that allude to hell:

Matthew 13:24–30

Matthew 13:47–50

Matthew 22:1–14

Matthew 25:31–46

3. List some of the most common images that Jesus used to describe hell (*Erasing Hell*, pages 76–80). What do you think these images are meant to convey?

4. Jesus used images to prick our emotions and open up our imagination. He wants His Word to penetrate every fabric of our being! How do you respond emotionally to Jesus' images of hell?

Sometimes I get so used to reading the Bible that even passages about hell seem to fall flat before they penetrate my heart. After reading these passages, I sometimes yawn and move on to the next verse! Writing *Erasing Hell* forced me to look hard into these passages and study them in detail. I felt God grip me and convict me. So let's take a closer look at one passage in particular: Matthew 8:5–13. Let's slow down, meditate, ponder, and really unpack what Jesus was talking about. Read through this passage slowly.

5. Who was the man that Jesus was talking to? Why would it have been shocking to hear Jesus say of this man, "with no one in Israel have I found such faith" (8:10)?

6. What particular characteristic of Jesus did the man acknowledge? How would you explain this characteristic in your own words?

7. How did the man view his own status as he encountered Jesus?

8. Jesus didn't use the word *hell* here, but He used imagery that described hell. What is this imagery?

9. How does Jesus want us to respond to such words?

As you have seen, Jesus talked about hell quite often. He not only used the word *gehenna* to refer to hell, but He also used many other images to describe the same reality—eternal fire, outer darkness, weeping, and gnashing of teeth.

Of all the passages where Jesus referred to hell, Matthew 25:31–46 is one of the most important, since it speaks about the duration of hell. Christians have debated for centuries whether unbelievers will be punished *forever* in hell, or whether they will be *annihilated* in hell. This is a very tough issue, and it cannot be settled as clearly as I had previously thought. However, Matthew 25 does seem to suggest that unbelievers will be punished forever in hell. Also, some people use this passage to argue that hell is not a place of *punishment* but a place where the unbeliever will be *corrected*. Let's work through these issues in more detail.

10. Explain the difference between "punishment" and "correction." (You might check a dictionary.)

11. In *Erasing Hell* I gave three reasons why the Greek word *kolasis* means "punishment" and not "correction." Summarize in your own words these three arguments.

12. Do you buy these arguments? Discuss any you either don't understand or don't agree with.

13. I also argued that the Greek word *aionios* probably means "everlasting" here in Matthew 25 and not just a period of time (which may be long or short). Summarize in your own words the two reasons why I argued for this meaning.

Again, do you buy these arguments? Discuss any you either don't understand or don't agree with.

Sometimes the meaning of the Bible jumps off the pages. At other times, though, it takes a lot of study, thinking, and discussion to unpack what it means. Such is the case with Matthew 25. If the Bible is God's inspired Word—which it is!—then we should be eager to study it in depth, with vigor and precision. This is especially true when it comes to sensitive doctrines such as hell. We can't afford to be wrong on this one, because this is not just a doctrine; it's the *destiny* of many people.

I'm a bit surprised at how many harsh statements Jesus made about hell. We often picture Jesus walking around with a lamb over His shoulders, blessing young children. Jesus was certainly tender and compassionate, but He was also blunt and harsh at times—especially toward religious folk!

14. How has your view of Jesus changed after reading through His statements on hell?

15. What would you say to someone who says, "I don't like this harsh Jesus. Someone so willing for people to be punished in hell isn't someone I want to trust and follow"?

16. How might what you've explored in this session affect the way you pray, evangelize, or disciple others in the faith?

For me, this study of hell has created a greater sense of God's holiness and mystery. On the one hand, God is my friend, and He welcomes me *enthusiastically* into His throne room (Heb. 4:14–16). But on the other hand, God is infinitely more holy than I. His ways are much higher than mine (Isa. 55:8–9), and His love and justice are equally incomprehensible. Sometimes it takes a tough doctrine like hell to drive this home. Again, this isn't just a study of hell; it's a study about God—the all-sovereign, all-loving, all-powerful King of Creation!

Continue to pray, and continue to tremble (Isa. 66:2), as you embark further into God's Word in the following chapters.

Reflections on …
What Jesus Actually Said about Hell

SESSION 4

What Jesus' Followers Said about Hell

For more information on the material in this session, read chapter 4 of the book **Erasing Hell: What God Said about Eternity, and the Things We Made Up.**

In the last chapter, we saw that Jesus spoke frequently and vividly about hell. In this chapter, we observe that the New Testament writers also spoke about hell, though they tended to use different terms. Surprisingly, Paul never actually used the word *hell* in all of his thirteen letters. One might conclude that Paul didn't actually think much about hell. But would this be an accurate conclusion?

In fact, Paul referred to the fate of the wicked more than any other New Testament writer did. Though he never used the actual word *hell*, he did speak of "death" as the result of sin, whereby the wicked would "perish" or "be destroyed" by the "wrath" of God. The sinner, according to Paul, stands "condemned" and will be "judged" by God on account of his sin. And unless the sinner repents and turns to Christ, he will be "punished" by God when Christ returns. Paul described the fate of the wicked with words such as *perish, destroy, wrath, punish,* and others more than eighty times in his thirteen letters. To put this in perspective, Paul made reference to the fate of the wicked more times in his letters than he mentioned God's forgiveness, mercy, or heaven combined.

1. How are these statistics about word usage relevant to the question of whether Paul thought about hell?

Paul never used the word *hell*, but in 2 Thessalonians 1:5–10 he gave a vivid description of what's going to happen to unbelievers when Christ comes back. Some say that Paul was not talking about all unbelievers here, but only those who persecute the church. After all, chapter 1, verse 6 says that God will "repay with affliction *those who afflict you*." However, there are other phrases in this passage that seem to say that all unbelievers are in view.

2. Which phrases in 2 Thessalonians 1:5–10 suggest that Paul probably had all unbelievers in mind?

3. Do you agree with this interpretation (that Paul was referring to all unbelievers and not just those who persecute Christians)? Why, or why not?

In chapter 1, verse 8, Paul used the term *vengeance* (ESV, NKJV), *retribution* (NASB), or *punish* (NIV) for what God is going to inflict on those who don't know Him. Paul didn't mean that God is the cosmic egotist who has to get back at people who hurt His pride, or the cosmic narcissist who gets mad when He doesn't get His way, or the cosmic sadist who gets sick pleasure from others' pain. When we humans seek vengeance, these are all too often our motives, so it's easy to project those motives on to God when we read a word like this. But vengeance without egotism, narcissism, and sadism is simply justice: giving people the just consequence of their offenses.

4. How persuasive is that to you? Do you think it's possible for a good God to treat unbelievers with vengeance? Explain.

In the last chapter, we discussed two different Christian views on hell: eternal conscious torment and annihilation. The first chapter of 2 Thessalonians has been used in support for annihilation, since it refers to unbelievers suffering "eternal destruction" (1:9). In itself, this phrase could mean annihilation, not an ongoing punishment. The word *eternal* could mean that the destruction is final, not necessarily that unbelievers will endure an ongoing state of being destroyed. In fact, language of destruction is very common in Paul's letters when he referred to the fate of the wicked, which is why some Christians hold to an annihilationist position.

However, in the Bible, language of destruction does not always mean "cease to exist." It can mean "cease to function in its intended capacity." Several examples make this clear.

5. Look up the following passages, where things are "destroyed" or "perish," and describe whether these things are annihilated (they ceased to exist) or cease to function in their intended capacity.

Matthew 9:17

Matthew 26:6–8 (the word *waste* is the same Greek word for "destroy")

2 Peter 3:5–6

I know this is getting to be heavy, but it's an important point to understand. Let's sum up the point: *Although the New Testament uses language of destruction when referring to the fate of the wicked, this does not necessarily mean that they will be annihilated.* This doesn't settle the issue, however. There are many other biblical passages that seem to support eternal conscious torment and others annihilation.

6. Which view of hell makes more sense to you emotionally and logically: annihilation or eternal conscious torment? (I encourage you to be very honest with your answer. And be sure not to judge others for which view they prefer.)

Do you want my honest answer? Logically and emotionally, the annihilation position makes good sense to me. I often agonize over the thought that unbelievers may be suffering forever in hell and would love it if such a view was not in the Bible. In some ways, I was hoping to find the annihilation position to be true. After writing *Erasing Hell*, I did find more support for this view than I was expecting, but at the end of the day, the eternal conscious torment position seems to have more biblical support. We've already seen that Matthew 25:31–46 suggests that unbelievers will suffer "everlasting punishment." There are two other passages in the book of Revelation that also seem to support this view: Revelation 14:9–11 and 20:10–15.

7. Revelation 14:9–11 refers to God's "wrath" and "anger." How do you reconcile these characteristics of God with His love and mercy?

8. Read Revelation 14:9–11 and explain why you think this passage teaches eternal conscious torment or annihilation (see also pages 103–104 of *Erasing Hell*).

9. Read Revelation 20:10–15 and explain why you think this passage teaches eternal conscious torment or annihilation (see also pages 105–107 of *Erasing Hell*).

10. How do you respond emotionally to Revelation 14:9–11 and 20:10–15?

11. At this point, do you believe that the reality of hell as a place of punishment is clearly taught in the New Testament? If so, what does this say to you about God? If not, what leaves you still unconvinced?

These were some of the hardest passages to work through in writing the book. Not only are they difficult to interpret, but they also reveal a great distance between what I believe and how I live my life. Many Christians like me say we believe in hell. *But do we live like it?* Do we act, serve, speak, work, play, laugh, cry, pray, parent our kids, relate to our coworkers, spend our paychecks, and love our neighbors in such a way that reveals that we believe in the place that Revelation 14 and 20 describe?

12. If you have felt the same disconnect between what you believe and how you act, discuss your thoughts.

13. How can we live differently in light of hell, while maintaining the sense of joy that the Bible also talks about (Phil. 3:1; 4:4)?

I mention at the end of the chapter that I dread the question unbelievers sometimes ask: "Do you think I'm going to hell?" For some reason, I'm very reluctant to say yes, because I think this will come off as mean and harsh. However, I can't say no, because this would not be truthful. There's a good chance that you also have encountered this dilemma.

14. What is the best way to respond to an unbeliever who asks you, "Do you think I am going to hell?" Explain.

Take some time for prayer. Tell God what you really think and feel about hell and about Him in light of hell. If you're still struggling with questions, take those to Him. If you're moved to pray for unbelievers in your life, and for the way you interact with them, then spend some time praying for them. Most of all, ask God to draw your heart and mind closer to Him as you continue to wrestle with this doctrine. Again, the goal of this study is to pursue a more fervent and faithful walk with Jesus.

What Jesus' Followers Said about Hell

SESSION 5

What Does This Have to Do with Me?

For more information on the material in this session, read chapter 5 of the book Erasing Hell: What God Said about Eternity, and the Things We Made Up.

When Christians talk about hell, they usually assume that they're talking about matters that affect other people. After all, hell is the place where unbelievers go, not a place for Christians. And this is true. Christians—genuine followers of Jesus—will not go to hell. But this does not mean that the doctrine of hell is irrelevant for believers. I was shocked when I paid close attention to the contexts where Jesus and the apostles spoke of hell. Most of the time, they described hell in order to confront and challenge *those who think they are in*, not those who know they are out (unbelievers). Even though hell is a place for non-Christians, its truth is relevant for believers.

In almost every passage where hell is mentioned, the audience was either believers or those who thought they were serving God. The latter, of course, includes the Pharisees, who were the Jewish religious leaders of the day, many of whom didn't follow Jesus. But the point remains: They *thought* they were right with God.

Matthew 7:21–24 is one such passage. The word *hell* doesn't occur in this text, but Jesus did speak of the day of judgment ("that day," verse 22), when believers will enter the kingdom of heaven and unbelievers will be sent away by Jesus. Jesus was thinking of hell in this passage, even though He didn't use the term. And what a scary thought! I truly believe this is one of the most frightening passages in all of Scripture. Imagine showing up on judgment day, thinking you've been serving Jesus all your life, but when you get there, Jesus scratches His head and says, "I never knew you; depart from me, you workers of lawlessness" (v. 23). These are terrifying words.

Let's study this passage in more detail.

1. Who was Jesus talking to in Matthew 7:21–24? (See also Matt. 5:1–2.)

2. What do you think Jesus meant when He said, "I never knew you"?

3. What does the phrase *workers of lawlessness* mean? (Jesus said something similar in Luke 13:27.)

4. Matthew 7:15–20 is probably referring to the same type of people who are condemned to hell in 7:21–24. What did Jesus call these people in 7:15–20?

The people condemned in Matthew 7:21–24 clearly think they're on Jesus' side. In fact, they've done lots of miracles in Jesus' name. Earlier in Matthew 5:22, Jesus threatened hell to those who attack a fellow human with harsh words. And again, the audience is the same: those who claim to be following Jesus.

5. How do you reconcile Matthew 5:22 and 7:21–24, where confessing Christians are in view, with other passages, where believers are assured of their salvation? (You may consult the following passages that speak of assurance: John 10:28–29; Rom. 8:1; 1 Cor. 1:4–9; Phil. 1:6.)

In Matthew 8:5–13, Jesus smuggled a warning about hell into the context of racism and ethnocentrism. The word *ethnocentrism* means thinking your ethnicity is superior. It's subtler than racism, which is a blatant hatred of another race. In most churches (though unfortunately not all) racism has greatly diminished over the years. But ethnocentrism is alive and well in subtle ways, and Jesus often confronted it, especially in Matthew 8:5–13.

6. Describe how Jesus confronted ethnocentrism in Matthew 8:5–13.

7. Read Ephesians 2:11–16 and explain the purpose of the death of Christ as it relates to Jews and Gentiles.

The New Testament seeks to break down walls that separate Jews from Gentiles. In Jesus' day, Jews would accept Gentiles only if they became converts to Judaism and took on the Jewish way of life (circumcision, dietary restrictions, observance of the Sabbath, etc.). But Jesus and His followers taught that a person does not need to leave aside his ethnicity or culture in order to become a Christian. One simply needs to have faith in Christ, and *that alone* will save you. Paul said in Galatians 3:28 that "there is neither Jew nor Greek … for you are all one in Christ Jesus." We could put this in contemporary terms and say, "There is neither black nor white, Asian nor Latino; you are all one in Christ."

8. Do you think it's important for local churches to put a lot of time and energy in creating a multiethnic body? Why, or why not?

9. Would you consider the church that you are a part of multiethnic? (If one ethnicity makes up more than 80 percent of its congregants, then it's not multiethnic.) What aspects of your church either do or don't appeal to more than one ethnic group?

Sometimes geography hinders a church from being multiethnic, but sometimes it's our own inherent ethnocentricity—we are all prone to hang out with people like us! But it's a powerful demonstration of the gospel when the world looks in and sees a bunch of diverse people rallying together and celebrating every week. It causes them to ask, *Why do you guys do that? What is it that brings you all together?* And according to Revelation 5:9, Jesus intentionally died to redeem people "from every tribe and language and people and nation." Multiethnic churches are able to showcase that facet of God's redeeming work in powerful ways. Many churches are seeking to become more ethnically diverse, and it's proven to be a powerful witness for the gospel.

Many churches are also seeking fresh avenues for confronting poverty. This, too, is an important issue according to Jesus and the apostles. In fact, in Matthew 25:31–46 Jesus said that reaching out to the poor and marginalized is an important criterion for inheriting eternal life.

10. Read through this passage slowly. List the ways in which you are living out the things listed in 25:35–36.

11. If your answer to question 10 is blank, then are there any ways in which you *could* be feeding the hungry, giving drink to the thirsty, clothing the naked, etc., in your own context?

12. Do you think Jesus had in mind believers, unbelievers, or both when He said, "As you did it to one of the least of these my brothers, you did it to me" (Matt. 25:40)? Explain your answer.

I recently had an atheist email me and say that Matthew 25:31–46 shows that feeding the hungry and clothing the naked (and the other things listed) lead to eternal life, and it doesn't matter whether someone believes in Jesus. And in one sense, he's right about this passage: It never explicitly says that the "sheep" (the ones who inherit eternal life) "believe in" Jesus. The words *faith* or *believe* are not used.

13. How would you respond to this person? Does Matthew 25:31–46 really teach that good works can save you apart from faith in Jesus? Explain.

14. After discussing misplaced assurance of salvation, ethnocentrism, and lack of concern for the poor, how are you moved to pray? Is there anything for which you'd like to thank God? Ask for forgiveness? Ask for help? Take some time to do that.

Reflections on …

What Does This Have to Do with Me?

SESSION 6

What If God …?

For more information on the material in this session, read chapter 6 of the book **Erasing Hell: What God Said about Eternity, and the Things We Made Up.**

One of the most troubling of God's characteristics is His sovereignty—His right and ability to rule over all things. A loving God we like. A forgiving God we take pleasure in. Even a just God we can handle (as long as His justice looks like ours). But a sovereign God scares us. *Can God really do whatever He wants to do?*

The answer is both yes and no. Yes, God can do whatever He wants to do: "Our God is in the heavens; he does all that he pleases" (Ps. 115:3). But no, God cannot do something that goes against His character. He cannot sin, He cannot cease to exist, and so on. But then again, God would not *want* to do something that goes against His character, so the answer is really more yes than no—God really can and does do whatever He desires to do.

And this can be troubling, especially since we are living in a world filled with pain and suffering. One of the greatest dilemmas of the Christian faith, one that scholars have been wrestling with for centuries, is the so-called problem of evil. In a word, how can a loving and all-powerful God allow such evil in the world? Either He's not very loving or He's not all-powerful; otherwise, He would stop such evil, heal the hurting, and dry the tears of those living in misery.

1. Is there anything in your life that has raised this question in your mind? It could be a personal tragedy or simply looking at world events and wondering where God is in all of this. Please write down your answer and share with the group. I encourage you to be open and honest here, as much as you feel comfortable.

2. How did you cope (or how are you coping) with this tragedy? How did people help you through this issue, or what Scriptures did you turn to in order to find rest and encouragement from God? Or what Scriptures did you find particularly troubling as you dealt with this issue?

3. If you have read chapter 6 of *Erasing Hell*, what are one or two things in the chapter that helped you think through the problem of evil, or things that were especially difficult and troubling as you thought through this issue?

Chapter 6 of *Erasing Hell* was especially difficult to write. Francis and I worked through the issue in great detail and even wrote several drafts before we landed on the version that's now in the book. The problem was that we wanted people to come face-to-face with God's sovereignty and recognize that He has the right and ability to do whatever He wants. And yet in no way did we want to downplay the real pain and misery that people are going through. We didn't want to belittle people's pain and struggle with God's sovereignty and the problem of evil. This is a very difficult issue, both theologically and pastorally. But I believe that it's foundational not only for how we think of hell, but most of all how we think about God.

Romans 9:6–24 affirms God's sovereignty most clearly, so let's read through that passage slowly and discuss it. Verses 6–13 look back at Genesis and note that when God was shaping His chosen people, He kept choosing a younger son to inherit the promises rather than the eldest, which would have been traditional. He did this not because those younger sons deserved it, but to show that He—not human expectation—was in charge.

4. Then Paul raised a rhetorical question that was probably on the minds of his original readers. It certainly was on my mind when I first read Romans 9! "Is there injustice on God's part?" (9:14). Describe how Paul answered this question in verses 14–18.

5. Paul asked a similar question in verse 19: "Why does he still find fault? For who can resist his will?" Again, describe how Paul answered this question in verses 20–24.

6. In *Erasing Hell* (pages 130–131), we discuss Romans 9:22–23. With or without looking at the book, read these two verses again and explain what you think Paul wanted his readers to believe about God from this passage. It may be best to try to sum up your response in one or two sentences so that you can focus on the main point.

7. After reading Romans 9:6–24, describe your reaction, both emotional and intellectual. What does it do to your soul? Strike fear? Provide security? Instill awe and wonder? Cause doubt about whether you can love this God? Does it raise more questions in your mind? If so, what are they?

God's sovereignty is a characteristic that we need to embrace not only with our minds but also with our hearts. We need not just to agree that God is in control; we need to be able to cherish and embrace this truth. This does *not* mean that everything God does makes perfect sense to us. Many things that God does are difficult to comprehend, and that's okay. No, it's expected *and good.* I mean, can you imagine a God who was easy to figure out? Sometimes people aren't easy to figure out (married folks can chime in here), so if God were easy to figure out, then we'd all be in big trouble!

We need a God whose ways are beyond us and whose actions cannot be put into a nice little box. We need a God who blows our minds and surprises us at every turn. And this is the

God of the Bible. God is sovereign and loving; wrathful and caring; surprising and faithful; free to do whatever He pleases, yet bound by His own relentless desire to show mercy, compassion, and love toward undeserving people. Indeed, "He will wipe away every tear from their eyes" (Rev. 21:4), but for now we live in a sin-plagued fallen world, where misery and suffering are inevitable. And to show that He cares, God stepped into this world (out of His own free choice) to take part in this misery and suffering (out of His own free choice) in order to love and redeem people who were not asking for it (out of His own free choice), and *that's how* He will be able to wipe every tear from our eyes.

8. Can you follow a God who doesn't make sense to you? Explain.

The Bible discusses God's sovereignty all over the place, not just in Romans 9. In fact, the very opening chapter of the Bible, Genesis 1, screams out that God is in control of the whole universe. The final two chapters, Revelation 21–22, declare victory over all creation, as God ushers in a "new heaven and a new earth" (Rev. 21:1). And everything in between affirms that God is wonderfully in control.

9. (Optional) If you're up for more Bible study, read through the following passages that speak of God's sovereignty. For each one, sum up the main idea in one or two sentences.

Job 40:1–14

Psalm 2:1–6

Isaiah 40:27–31

Isaiah 46:8–11

Romans 11:33–36

God is in control, and we are not. This may be tough to handle, especially if you're a control freak like me! It's hard to give up our own sovereignty and lay it at God's feet. It's one thing to acknowledge that God is in control in a general sense, but it's another thing to believe that God is in charge of the nitty-gritty details of my life: my bank account, my job (or lack thereof), my relationships, my family, my ministry, my health, my house. God has given us these things, and God may take them away. But following Job's example, we must bless and worship the name of the Lord through thick and thin (Job 1:21–22). This is the posture that the Creator delights in among His creatures. And yet I'll be the first one to admit that this can be *very* difficult.

10. Are there things in your life (job, family, health, money) that you have not trusted God to rule over? Are there things in your life that are causing you great anxiety? If so, what are those things?

As we close this chapter, it may be good to pray through some of the items that you listed in question 10. Pray that God would help you to stop holding on to things that belong to Him. Ask Him to take away the anxiety that rules your heart and dictates your behavior. Beg God to help you trust His sovereignty over your finances, job, marriage, kids, or anything else that you are anxious about. And if His sovereignty itself—His power to do whatever He wants that is consistent with His character—makes you anxious, talk with Him about the things you're afraid He might do, or the things He's already done that are hard for you to accept.

Reflections on …
What If God …?

SESSION 7

Don't Be Overwhelmed

For more information on the material in this session, read chapter 7 and Appendix 1 (Frequently Asked Questions) of the book **Erasing Hell: What God Said about Eternity, and the Things We Made Up.**

This has been a heavy topic! Both Francis and I often say that *Erasing Hell* was the most difficult piece we've written, and probably the most difficult we will ever write. Studying, meditating on, and being challenged by the doctrine of hell can take the wind out of your sails and ruin your day. And in one sense, *this is good*. If you live in America like I do, then you can agree that our culture is addicted to comfort, ease, and the pursuit of pleasure. If we are cold, we crank up the heat. If we're hot, we blast the AC. If we get a headache, we immediately pop a pill. If we feel depressed, we pop another pill. Much of our time and energy is spent pursing comfort and numbing pain. And so when we encounter a doctrine that brings *discomfort*, our immediate reaction is to turn the page, close the book, or just think about something else.

But sometimes it's good—spiritually *healthy*—to linger for a while on the more uncomfortable things in life. The fact is, not everything is peaches and cream. Suffering is a reality. People *are* depressed. Suicide rates are on the rise. And real people are *really going to a place of torment called hell*. We can't ignore this. We can't just go through life and pretend that the

Bible doesn't talk about hell. Not only would this be dishonest, but it would also be spiritually *unhealthy*. If there's cancer in the bones, then we need to do something about it. And there's a cancer in the bones of every human. It's called sin, and the outcome is eternal death in hell. To turn a blind eye would be foolish and unloving.

So I hope this study has helped instill in you a sobering sense that life is not a gigantic playground, not even in America. We need to let the doctrine of hell simmer in our hearts. We need it to aggravate our will and fester in our minds to help shock us out of complacency. This is what it has done to my own soul, so if I've been able to share the misery, then the book has been a success!

But that's not the full picture. Christianity is not all about doom and gloom. It's driven by joy, victory, and celebration. Paul commanded the Philippians to "rejoice in the Lord" (Phil. 3:1). And just in case they forgot, he commanded them again in the next chapter: "Rejoice in the Lord *always*; again I will say, Rejoice" (Phil. 4:4). He told the Thessalonians that they were his "glory and joy" (1 Thess. 2:20). David told God that "in your presence there is fullness of joy; at your right hand are pleasures forevermore" (Ps. 16:11), and God rebuked the Israelites for not serving Him "with joyfulness and gladness of heart, because of the abundance of all things" (Deut. 28:47).

Hell is real. Life is filled with suffering. But God's presence and His bountiful creation should elicit joy from our hearts.

So *don't be overwhelmed*. Let the doctrine of hell shock you out of complacency, but don't let it steal your joy.

1. Which end of the spectrum do you lean toward? Do you emphasize the seriousness or playfulness of life? Does thinking about God and the world make you more joyful or solemn, happy or sad? Explain.

2. What does it look like to be able to "rejoice in the Lord always" and yet embrace the horrifying picture of hell found in the Bible?

3. What step can you take toward balance between seriousness and joy?

Living out this tension is tough. I've gone through phases of my life when I was out of balance. Either I was too playful—that's how I got into surfing!—or I was too serious and didn't let the joy of the Lord rule my heart. Perhaps you, too, have been reminded of the seriousness of life by reflecting on hell.

This study of hell may have also raised more intellectual and theological questions in your mind about hell. And this is why I included an appendix of Frequently Asked Questions about hell, with the answers Francis and I gleaned from Scripture. For the rest of this session, I'd like you to discuss those questions. You can work through them all, or you can pick two or three that interest you the most. If you have the book, you may consult it as much as you like.

Please note: I don't want you to just quote what I say in the book. I want you to think through the material, sum it up in your own words, add your own thoughts, and even disagree with what I say if you feel that you have a better, more biblical, response. These questions are meant to foster discussion and reflection, not show off your ability to copy what I say.

4. Are the images of fire, darkness, and worms to be understood literally? (See, for example, Matt. 13:42; 18:8–9; Jude 7, 13; Rev. 14:10–11; 20:10, 15.) Why, or why not?

5. Are there degrees of punishment in hell? In other words, will every unbeliever suffer equally in hell, or will some suffer worse than others?

6. Is hell at the center of the earth? If not, then *where is it?*

7. Does the Old Testament word *sheol* refer to hell? (See, for example, Gen. 37:35; 42:38; Isa. 14:11; 38:10; Num. 16:30.)

8. What about the person who has never heard the gospel? Does that person automatically inherit eternal life? Why, or why not?

How do you feel about that? Does it seem fair?

9. Did Jesus preach to people in hell between His death and resurrection? If so, where do we see this?

10. How can God be loving and still send people to hell?

11. These aren't all the questions that surround the doctrine of hell—there are hundreds more. If you have other questions about hell that you wish to discuss with your group, then list them below. For the sake of time, try to pick the top two or three.

12. Where has this study taken you? For instance, are you motivated to share the gospel with unbelievers? Or do you feel distanced from a God whom you don't understand?

As you wrap up this study, let's pray through this material one more time. Prayer is essential for any Bible study. It helps bridge the gap between heart and mind, and it recognizes that we need the Creator's help to live out these truths. Here are some things you may want to pray for:

Father, compel me to live differently, think differently, feel differently, about You. May my view of You be magnified a thousand times as a result of this study.

Jesus, thank You for rescuing me from hell by taking on my hell through the cross. Let my gratitude for the cross compel me to speak to others about Your beautiful redeeming grace.

Spirit, cleanse my soul from all apathy and complacency. Help me to live more passionately and faithfully in light of hell.

Reflections on …
Don't Be Overwhelmed

Notes for Discussion Leaders

A small group working through this material will benefit from having a discussion leader. If that's you, don't worry—you don't need to have all the answers. This workbook is discussion-driven, not teacher-driven. All you need is the willingness to prepare each week, guide the discussion, and rely on the Holy Spirit to work in your heart and the hearts of group members. This study can give you hands-on experience in depending not on your natural leadership abilities but on the Spirit. If you pray for His help, He will give it.

Discussion Leader's Job Description

The discussion leader's job isn't to have all the answers. He or she simply needs to:

- Keep the group on track when it's tempted to go off on a tangent.
- Keep the discussion moving so that it doesn't get stuck on one question.
- Make sure that everyone gets a chance to talk and that no one dominates. (It is not necessary that every person respond aloud to every question, but every person should have the chance to do so.)
- Make sure that the discussion remains respectful.

the Discussion

er, you'll probably want to read the chapters from *Erasing Hell* before
ork through your own responses to the discussion questions ahead of
e the meeting, be sure the chairs are arranged so that everyone can see
one another.

Guiding the Discussion

A few ground rules can make the discussion deeper:

- *Confidentiality:* Whatever is said in the group stays in the group. Nothing is to be repeated to those who weren't there.
- *Honesty:* We're not here to impress each other. We're here to grow and to know each other.
- *Respect:* Disagreement is welcome. Disrespect is not.

The discussion should be a conversation among the group members, not a one-on-one with the leader. You can encourage this with statements like, "Thanks, Allison. What do others of you think?" or, "Does anyone have a similar experience, or a different one?"

Don't be afraid of silence—it means group members are thinking about how to answer a question. Trust that the Spirit is working in the members of your group, and wait. Sometimes it's helpful to rephrase the question in your own words. Then wait for others' responses, and avoid jumping in with your own.

I recommend discussing the numbered questions in order. Read each question aloud, and ask the group to respond. It's not necessary to go around the circle and let everyone answer every question. That can get boring. Instead, have a few people share their thoughts. You can ask follow-up questions (such as "Why?" or "What do you think about that?" or "What do the rest of you think?") to stimulate a challenging conversation.

Feel free to have someone read a portion of *Erasing Hell* out loud whenever that seems helpful. I obviously think that what I've said there makes sense, but your group should be a place where people feel free to ask questions for clarification or even to outright disagree with me. I would hate for people to sit silent, nod their heads, and go away confused, unconvinced, unheard, or unchanged. Hell can be a distressing topic. Don't be in such a hurry to get through the material that there isn't time for people to voice their unpopular thoughts and painful emotions. (At the same time, be willing to step in if someone tends to dominate the discussion or says things that are hurtful to others.)

The answers to the questions are important, but I am most concerned that people may study Jesus and never *know* Him, never be *changed* by Him. With every session, keep asking yourself and your group: "How should this change us? If we really submitted our lives to Jesus and opened ourselves up to what He says about hell, what would He have us do? Where would He have us go?" At the end of the day, it's about laying hold of the power of the Spirit in order to accomplish what God has placed us on this earth to do. It's about advancing the kingdom of God. It's about His will being done on earth as in heaven.

Most of all, spend time praying for your group. You can't talk anyone into a wholehearted devotion to God. Some of the truths your group will face in this study will be hard to understand. Those that are understood may be difficult to embrace. You'll need to pray hard as for your group. You should also pray as a group and ask God to help you comprehend the reality and seriousness of hell, and then for His strength to respond to the doctrine with reverence and zeal. May God accomplish the extraordinary in your lives as you seek to follow Jesus—even as you reflect on the doctrine of hell.

Session 1

Question 1. Some group members may know a lot about what the Bible teaches. Others may have a picture of hell shaped mainly by pop culture: red devils with horns and tails, for example. This is a chance to get all of those mental pictures out on the table. Likewise, some group members may have grown up around hellfire preachers, while others may have grown up laughing at comical portrayals of hell. Because our baggage affects us in ways we often aren't aware of, everyone will benefit from having it out in the open. Also, group members will have more empathy for one another if they understand where others have come from. You might consider going around the group circle and giving each person a minute or two to share the way hell was depicted to them when they were growing up. (Do limit people to two minutes, because some could go on all night about this.)

Question 2. If answers to question 1 reflect mainly cultural baggage, answers here may reflect distortions about God. Give people a chance to voice those. It's good to get distortions out in the open. You can close this sharing by saying something like, "Over the course of this study we're going to have a chance to compare our views of hell and of God with what the Bible says." You may want to write down some of the distorted views and then come back to them at the end of session 7 so group members can talk about how their ideas have or haven't changed.

Question 3. It's extremely important to set an example of honesty here. Don't let any preachy group members discourage others from sharing their honest difficulties with hell. The Bible is going to speak for itself in this study, and people need to know that this is a safe place to say what they really think. You may need to be ready here to share your honest discomfort with some of what the Bible says about hell, so be sure to think about this before the group meets.

Question 5. God's moral will involves the values that please Him. He lets people disobey these values. However, His decreed will is the events that He causes to happen. He let Samson disobey His moral will about pagan women, but He used the situation to carry out His decreed will to defeat the Philistines. If group members don't get this, you can slow down and look at Judges 14 to see how these two factors played out.

Question 6. Invite the group to pray for these people by name in your prayer time at the end of the meeting.

Question 9. To gnash one's teeth is to grind them together. It's a sign of strong anger or pain. It may also reflect people's continual rebellion in hell, as they gnash their teeth in anger at God. Weeping suggests deep sorrow.

Question 10. Jesus isn't literally ignorant about anyone. He's using a figure of speech to describe a lack of intimate relationship, the kind of relationship where people lower their deceptive barriers and know each other's hearts and histories.

Be sure to allow plenty of time at the end of each group meeting for members to pray about the people they named in question 6, as well as for themselves. In your prayers, set an example of honesty before God and desire to let His words change you.

Session 2

Question 1. This question will probably elicit different responses, depending on the ethnicity of the group members or their upbringing. Be sensitive to any racially charged discussions that might erupt. The main point of this question is to reveal how we often imagine Jesus in our own minds in ways that reflect ourselves or our upbringing.

Question 3. This is a straightforward question that should be easily answered if one understands the main point of chapter 2 in *Erasing Hell*. The simple point: First-century Jews believed in hell. If Jesus didn't, He would have no problem disagreeing with them. This sets up the main point of chapter 3: Jesus didn't disagree with them. As a leader, it would be good for you to emphasize how important this argument is for believing that Jesus really did speak of a literal hell.

Question 4. A follow-up question you may ask is: "Does the image of fire refer to God *refining* the wicked to make them fit for heaven, or to God *punishing* the wicked for their sin?" This is important, because many people who deny that hell is for punishment say that the image of fire conveys *correction* and *refinement*, rather than *punishment*. To discuss this possibility, you can look at the passage in question 2, as well as other passages from chapter 2 of *Erasing Hell*. Those passages are all from nonbiblical sources; in chapter 3 you'll look at the Gospels. You can keep this question in mind and come back to it: Does this image of fire sound like *refinement* or *punishment*? How can we tell?

The image of darkness conveys separation, and lamenting refers to suffering and pain.

Question 6. The difference between annihilation and eternal conscious torment is a very important one, and it'll come up at various times throughout the rest of this study. So be sure that everyone understands the difference. If it's clear to you, don't assume that it's clear to everyone. Be sure to explain the difference even if it seems very simple. Annihilation means the person ceases to exist, so the torment ceases. Annihilation isn't much different from what many atheists believe happens when you die: Dying can be terribly painful, but when it's over, you cease to exist.

Question 7. This could spark a heated discussion. Some people are adamant that the suffering *must* be forever in order for it to be just. Vice versa, most annihilationists are appalled that anyone could embrace eternal conscious torment. At this point, establish that each view may be valid, but the most important thing is what the Bible says. I recommend gently challenging those who think that the suffering must be forever. On the flip side, if some think that annihilation makes more sense, make sure that the group allows for them to think this way. We'll explore the Bible in the next few chapters to see which view is more correct, so at this point it's good to just let people discuss how they feel about the matter. You may also want to end this discussion by asking people to believe what the biblical text will end up saying about the matter.

Question 8. See pages 57–61 in *Erasing Hell.*

Question 11. This question could spark a lot of discussion, but because it's near the end of the session, you may be pressed for time. Try to limit people's answers to either a couple of minutes or a couple of questions. Some may have a good forty-five minutes' worth of questions to discuss. You can assure them that many of these will be answered in the rest of the study and that they will have a chance to raise their questions later if they aren't addressed here. You can have someone write down a list of everyone's questions so that you can come back to them in session 7 to see which ones haven't yet been addressed. Or you can ask everyone to write down their own questions and bring them back in session 7 unless they come up before then.

Question 13. Let people be honest here, but gently challenge those who are way off in their response—for example, if some say that hell should be the only thing we preach to unbelievers, or that we should never bring it up.

Session 3

Question 1. This taps into the same question raised in question 3 of session 2. If the group is still in the fog over the argument, then it may be good to explain it again.

Question 2. This question could take up a lot of time, so try to be efficient in how you manage it. Most groups should spend only a few minutes on each passage, and some will want to leave this question for individual study. If your time is limited, I wouldn't let this question go longer than ten minutes in order to allow sufficient time for the rest of this session. I've included this question mainly so that people need not feel that we're discussing only those passages that support my view. If yours is a group that wants to do its own digging and come to its own conclusions, this is a chance to do so.

Question 4. Again, you'll need to set the tone of honesty here. Some may be scared of "saying the wrong thing," but this question is designed not to confront their emotions but to reveal them. It's important to be honest with how we *feel* about the doctrine so that we can ultimately let the text influence and shape our feelings.

Question 5. The man was a centurion, a Roman military leader. The term *centurion* (think "century") may have meant that he was a leader of one hundred soldiers. At the very least, he was high up in the military and also in his social class. For Jews in Palestine, Rome was the symbol of oppression, opposition, and godlessness. Jesus' encounter with this man was the ultimate—and most shocking—example of loving one's enemy.

Question 6. His authority. That is, His *right* and *power* to tell people what to do and to decide how things are going to go. You don't need to spend a lot of time on this question, but the issue of Jesus' (and the Father's) authority or sovereignty will be a recurring theme in our discussion of hell.

Question 7. Even though the centurion also had much authority, when compared to Jesus he recognized that Jesus' authority was infinitely greater.

Question 8. "Thrown into the outer darkness. In that place there will be weeping and gnashing of teeth" (Matt. 8:12). This imagery is used elsewhere to speak of hell.

Question 10. "Punishment" is straightforward—it's retribution for sin. We do something bad, and we get punished for our disobedience. "Correction" refers to making a bad person *good*. It's similar to cleansing or refinement. So those who think that hell is for "correction" and not for "punishment" believe that those who go there will ultimately have a chance to accept Jesus, get out of hell, and enter eternal life.

Questions 11 and 12. Make sure you allow people to disagree, but gently guide and correct them if there are some passages that conflict with their views. You want to create an arena where people can be honest, but you also don't want to breed heresy and bad logic.

Session 4

Question 2. The main phrase is: "those who do not know God and on those who do not obey the gospel of our Lord Jesus" (2 Thess. 1:8). You can also point out that the "punishment of eternal destruction" (v. 9) is a common description of the fate of unbelievers, and in other passages it isn't limited to those who persecute the church (Matt. 18:8–9; 1 Cor. 15:25–26; 2 Pet. 2:12). You can add, though, that there may be degrees of punishment in hell and that those who persecute the church *may* receive a harsher torment in hell. This isn't crystal clear in the text, but it may get people thinking and eager to search the Scriptures—always a good thing!

Question 4. If people have a problem with the term *vengeance*, then it may be good to walk through the paragraph prior to this question. It lays out the logic of "vengeance" in a healthy way. Are there pieces of this paragraph that people don't agree with? You can also talk about how vengeance is related to justice. What is justice? Does vengeance seem like something different? If so, how are they different if we take away all of the egotism, narcissism, and sadism that can make human vengeance unjust? Is it inherently cruel and unjust to give people what they deserve if that is something less than eternal bliss or painlessly ceasing to exist? Without badgering people into submission, you can explore the emotions and logic behind people's concerns about the biblical teaching.

Question 5. Be aware that people may be using different translations and therefore have a little trouble with this question. I'm using the ESV, but the NASB, NIV, or NKJV will render the passages with similar words. Other translations, such as *The Message* or *Living Bible*, may prevent some from answering this question adequately.

Question 6. People's responses may be driven by sheer emotion or by theological reasoning. For instance, some theologians in the past have said: "An infinite crime against an infinite God demands an infinite punishment." Therefore, never-ending torment is a theological necessity. If the discussion isn't lively, you may think about throwing this formulation out there to see what people think. As always, point them back to the Bible to see if such formulations can be defended from Scripture.

Questions 7–10. These passages in Revelation contain a good deal of images that aren't necessarily to be taken literally. For instance, the "wine of God's wrath" and "cup of his anger" (Rev. 14:10) aren't literal beverages. But some people dismiss much of what Revelation says on hell since it's nothing more than images that aren't literal. However, if this comes up, you may want to point out that even symbolic images are meant to convey a literal truth, even if the image itself isn't literal. For instance, the "cup of his anger" isn't a literal cup, but it is an image meant to say something about God. It emphasizes God's real anger in a vivid, poetic way. So with all the images, we need to ask what literal truth they convey.

Question 12. Again, you'll foster much more honesty and discussion if you lead the way in being honest here.

Session 5

Question 1. He was talking to His disciples, as Matthew 5:1–2 makes clear (Jesus had the same people in view in the whole Sermon on the Mount, Matthew 5–7). The crowds were also looking on (Matt. 5:1–2), so Jesus may have an eye on them as well, but the main point is that He was speaking to *those who are in* and not *those who are out* (those who don't follow Jesus) in Matthew 7:21–24.

Question 2. See the note to question 10 of session 1.

Question 3. This is a straightforward question, and the parallel in Luke 13 will help, since there Jesus called them "workers of evil." The reason why I direct people to this question is to point out that these are *lawless, evil* people. They have blatant, ongoing, visible sin in their lives. So the typical Christian who is trying to obey God, whose basic posture is one of obedience, should not live in an unhealthy fear that Jesus doesn't know him or her. This passage should sober us up, but it shouldn't strike an unhealthy fear in the hearts of those living a life of obedience, repentance, and faith. Feel out your group, and be sure to give assurance where assurance is needed.

Question 4. "False prophets ... in sheep's clothing" (v. 15). Again, these aren't Christians who struggle with sin, but people deliberately manipulating the gospel for their own benefit.

Question 5. This question is *very* important and could take hours to hash out. But it's extremely practical, so I recommend taking a good bit of time discussing it. It'll be helpful to look at the passages in the parentheses in good detail beforehand to be prepared to lead the discussion. One thing you may want to talk about is what it means to have saving faith in Christ. Is going through the motions of a five-minute sinner's prayer once in one's life enough, or is there more to faith than that? Does faith mean mentally agreeing with a list of statements about Jesus? The Greek word for *faith* is the same as the Greek word for *faithfulness*, so some would say real faith includes surrender to Christ and a desire to be faithful to Him—that is, to obey Him.

Question 6. Jesus contrasted the Gentile getting saved with the Jews ("sons of the kingdom"— Matt. 8:12) who rejected the gospel. The original audience would have been struck by how Jesus tapped into very sensitive racial issues between Jews and Gentiles. These racial tensions are paralleled today in our own racial conflicts, which Jesus seeks to resolve through the cross.

Question 7. This is a very important though neglected passage. In short, it says that one of the purposes of Christ's death was to establish racial unity between Jews and Gentiles. By implication, this would include racial unity of all sorts who follow Jesus. If you want more material on this subject, you may want to view my message on this passage, preached at Cornerstone Church in November 2010. It's titled "The Gospel of Reconciliation." You can view it here: http://prestonsprinkle.com/media.php?pageID=23.

Question 12. In the book of Matthew, the phrase *brothers of mine* refers to believers, not all poor people in general. So Matthew is saying that believers must take care of other poor and oppressed believers. I don't think that you can fulfill this passage by simply giving money to every homeless person you meet.

Question 13. This is a very difficult theological issue. A good way to approach this question will be to focus on the message of Matthew as a whole. We cannot read Matthew 25 in isolation from everything else the book teaches, and the book as a whole (along with Mark, Luke, and John) emphasizes faith in Jesus as a necessary prerequisite for good works. You could read through John 3 for evidence.

Session 6

Questions 1–2. Be aware that these are difficult theological and emotional issues that have no easy answer. It will be good to be open and honest here, but some things may be too difficult for people to discuss in this group, especially if they don't know other group members well. This is okay. Encourage the group to be honest, but don't force people to talk about things that they're not ready to explore.

Questions 4–7. This passage can be difficult to read and believe. The natural theological question that comes up is election (or predestination) and free will (or human choice). If the group wants to discuss these things and you feel comfortable leading them through it, then this may be a good place. However, these aren't the primary issues I want to dive into at this point. I would like the group to wrestle with God's sovereignty in broader terms, not necessarily figure out the interrelationship between divine and human involvement in salvation. But feel out your group members and discuss what's most pressing to them.

Question 6. The main point is to see that Paul was not making a dogmatic theological assertion here, but wanted his audience to affirm that the Creator has the right to do whatever He pleases, even if it doesn't sit well with us.

Question 8. You may want to read *Erasing Hell* pages 21–22, where I discuss a similar issue.

Question 9. This is optional, since Romans 9 may be heavy enough to tackle. However, if your group is eager for more, or is really struggling with Romans 9, then looking at these other passages may be helpful.

Question 10. Again, you'll need to take the lead in being honest here.

Session 7

Questions 1–3. These are all important ideas to work through. I don't normally like the word *balance*, but in this regard I think it's important to balance seriousness with joy. To add some theological shape to this question, you may want to discuss the so-called "already/not yet" tension that we live in. In other words, we look back on Christ's victory on the cross ("already"), and yet we long for His second coming, where He will finish the job ("not yet"). So we have reason both to celebrate (the cross) and weep (longing for His second coming). I think this very tension allowed Paul to rejoice and weep throughout his ministry.

Question 4-10. These are all straight out of the book, so be sure to read through the Frequently Asked Questions in detail to help guide the discussion. Allow people the freedom to think freely, yet encourage biblical responses in the discussion.

Question 10. This is a particularly difficult question, and my answer in the book only scratches the surface.

"Crazy Love may just be the most challenging book outside of God's Word you will read this year."

It's crazy, if you think about it. The God of the universe loves you with a radical, unconditional, self-sacrificing love. And what is our typical response? We go to church, sing songs, and try not to cuss. God is calling you to a passionate love relationship with Himself. Because the answer to religious complacency isn't working harder at a list of do's and don'ts—it's falling in love with God.

Experience God's crazy love with Francis Chan's book and DVD study resource.

Watch free videos for each chapter at www.CrazyLoveBook.com

To learn more visit our Web site or a Christian bookstore near you.

eternity bible college

Rigorous – because God deserves our best

Affordable – because an elite Bible education shouldn't burden people with debt

Bible-Focused – because the Bible is foundational for faith and life

Engaged – because Jesus calls us to minister to the world around us

Church-Centered – because the church is Jesus' bride

Taste and See – We offer "Introduction to Discipleship Counseling," a life-transforming course on applying the Scriptures to your life and the lives of others, for credit with no application, no obligation, and no cost. It is 100% free.

Classes are offered both onsite in Simi Valley, CA and online.

We offer a Bachelors of Biblical Studies as well as several Certificate Programs.

EBC exists to glorify God through graduates whose lives are transformed by rigorous study of the Bible as Scripture, impassioned love for God, and gracious service in the church for the world.

For More Information…

www.EternityBibleCollege.com
admissions@EternityBibleCollege.com
telephone: 805.900.3761

"Training people to live and die well."

~Francis Chan
founder 2004